Disrupt the Workday; 18 hours 18 Days, 18 Adventures

First Edition

Teri McElrath

ISBN 978-1-63844-008-6 (paperback)
ISBN 978-1-63844-009-3 (digital)

Christian Faith Publishing, Inc.
832 Park Avenue
Meadville, PA 16335
www.christianfaithpublishing.com

Printed in the United States of America

To my sister Shanell, my best friend Lisa, my grandmothers Dee and Rosa, and my parents Liane and Miguel

I ensured that I planned my workday around the adventure instead of planning the adventure around the workday.

—Teri McElrath

CONTENTS

CHAPTER 1

The Experiment

It was the summer of 2018, and the company that I worked for had just announced that we were being acquired. My heart hit the bottom of my stomach. I became overwhelmed for a moment by the fear of loss of another job. What was I going to do?

After reading the announcement on the radiated screen, I paused. This narrative was all too familiar. I recalled how I felt five years earlier when I worked at another company. I received an unexpected text message from the CEO at seven a.m. She announced that we sold our wireless spectrum. I remember looking out of the window at the lakefront while I listened to that conference call. A tear ran down my face. I had spent six years at that company. I realized that vicious cycles were repeating themselves.

Time was not my own. Years lapsed and I found myself in the same situation that I was in five years before. Nothing had changed. I was living the movie *Groundhog Day*. I was not living life deliberately. The minutes, hours, days, weeks, months, and years—where did the time go? How did I get here?

After a couple of bouts with my health, I realized that time is the most precious commodity. I did a personal assessment and realized that there were not many years left on my timeline. I needed to make the most of it. I no longer wanted to be a slave to the clock. I also realized that there was a gap, very few hours to experience life during the week.

Routine was killing me, my creativity, and stealing hours from my timeline. How could I break the routine and make more time for adventure and exploration? Why should I wait 'til I save monies for an exotic trip? Why do I have to wait to get approval from my supervisor for time off from work?

In America, we are conditioned to work a traditional nine-to-five job. We are subjected to an oppressive schedule. By the end of the workday, we are burned out. We spend time with our family and friends after 5:00 p.m. or on the weekends. Hours of joy are limited to happy hours, brunches, or vacation destinations. This seemed unfair to me. There must be a way to take control of the hours every day to break the routine and remind myself that I am human.

This gave birth to the start of a personal journey to disrupt the workday, break the cycle. An experiment to reclaim hours lost due to the daily grind of life. I live in a city that I never have time to enjoy. There is so much life around me, but I only have a few hours to enjoy it. I was on a mission to take back one hour per day to live deliberately. During this hour, I would step out of my comfort zone to learn something new and fuel an adrenaline rush, an out of body experience. Thirty days, thirty adventures, thirty hours. I planned a list of activities that I could complete within one hour.

One summer day, when it was time, I grabbed my backpack. I flew through the revolving doors and never looked back. Taking that first step was uncomfortable, but it set me free! This book is a preview of the results of this personal experiment I call the "Deliberate Lunch!" The goal was to prove the theory that you can break away in the middle of the day and live. I proved by the end of the experiment that you can slow down the clock and live deliberately! My friends and family were inspired by the journey. I hope that you are too!

Thirty Days, Thirty Hours, Thirty Adventures

It was simple. In the summer of 2018, I generated a list of adventures that I wanted to experience. Once I had the list, I incorporated these activities into my daily calendar. It was a bit overwhelming at first. There was so much that I wanted to experience. I knew that I liked museums, nature, technology, poetry, and live music.

So I searched the web for activities that fell into these categories to help me organize. The criteria was that these adventures had to be experienced during the lunch hour. If I ran a little over, that was okay. I ensured that I planned my workday around the adventure instead of planning the adventure around the workday. Any work meetings that I scheduled could not interfere with my deliberate lunch experience. The schedule was agile just in case there were unforeseen circumstances like weather inclement. I blocked the time off the calendar so that colleagues knew that I was unavailable.

It felt strange at first blocking time on my calendar, but I had to remember that the goal was to gain control over the clock and not to let the clock control me. It took me a few days to finalize my calendar. I set a date then started my adventures. When I returned to the office, I shared my stories with my colleagues. It felt so good to have stories to share at the end of the workday!

Here is what happened:

1. I made a list of the categories of activities that I enjoy.
2. I took the time to research activities and events in the area.
3. I created a list of events that met my criteria.
4. I incorporated the events into my daily calendar.
5. I journaled daily before bedtime.
6. I shared my adventures with my friends, colleagues, and family.

"What if I fall?"
"Oh, but Darling, what if you fly?"
—Erin Hanson

How to Use This Book

This is a tool to help you reclaim your life by redesigning every day! Instead of planning for a typical workday, plan to break the routine. Your journey will include eighteen adventures, eighteen hours, and eighteen days of self-discovery. There is so much more to life. Take a moment, slow down. What do you see around you? How can you make each day more meaningful?

You will find snippets from my journal and some ideas on how to get started. First you can use this book as a guide to complete the adventures shared here, or you can create a list of your own.

Secondly, there is no right or wrong way to go about it. This book is to inspire you to live a deliberate life. Of course, geographically, the adventures will look a little different, and that's okay.

Finally, don't pressure yourself to venture out every day. If you start with just one day a week, you will start to feel a lot better. The goal is to end your work week with amazing stories to share. Hopefully the ideas shared here can be used by all.

The book is intended to be interactive. There are some moments where you will need to take the time to reflect and journal. Why are you embarking on this journey? Be sure to capture how you are feeling the moment. What did you see, hear, or smell? What did you learn about yourself? What are some initial reactions to the change in lifestyle? To keep you motivated and inspired, there are some breaks for story times and inspirational quotes. Use this book as a reminder of the day you took a leap of faith to be happy! Keep it close to your heart.

Getting Started

The first step is to reflect on why you want to embark on this journey. What do you want to gain from this experience? How many hours do you want to recapture in your life? Start with a small goal like one hour per week. Don't overwhelm yourself. Change is always difficult. It is not easy taking the first step.

There were so many times that I talked myself out of it. I thought that one hour was not going to be enough time. What are my colleagues going to think? What if my activities interfere with my work? At some point, I had to decide what was best for me.

You may go through the same process. Don't worry, this is normal. After some personal reflection and setting your goals, do an assessment of your work schedule. When do you take your breaks? What day of the week can you break away? I would then recommend blocking time on your calendar. If this is the lunch hour, block this time off indefinitely. This will remind you that this time is for you. It will also send a message to others in the organization that you are unavailable during this time.

Thirdly, start to assess the environment around your work. Is it the fall, winter, spring? What events or activities are planned during these seasons? Are there museums around you? Is there a public park or beach? Start jotting down things that you would like to experience. Once you have your list, integrate these events into your daily calendar. This small change, adding something to your calendar that brings you joy, will immediately start to shift your perspective. You will start to get more excited about the workday! Instead of worrying about tasks and meetings, you will be focused on what you need to do to prepare for your adventure!

Finally, the most challenging hurdle that you will need to overcome is fear. There is always fear of the unknown. Living a more deliberate life requires a shift in mindset. It requires that you take care of yourself and tend to your needs. This is difficult in a noisy, distracted world that is requiring so much of your time, energy, and attention. Don't worry, you are not alone. The next few chapters will provide you with some ideas. You can complete these adventures, or plan some of your own. Whatever you decide, the goal is to start your own journey! Disrupt your workday!

Why do you want to embark on this journey?

Reflect here

Sing like no one is listening, love like you have never been hurt, dance like no one is watching, and live like it is heaven on earth.

—Mark Twain

CHAPTER 2

Hour 1

Adventure 1: Try Bubble Tea or Baklava!

There is a melting pot of different races, cultures, ethnicities, and religions around us. Today, plan to learn something about a different culture. On day one, my first adventure was a visit to Chinatown. It had been a while since I visited. It may sound funny, but I had never had bubble tea. I am also a fan of Chinese medicine, so learning more about how herbs can heal the body is a passion. This was the perfect outing for me.

I researched a juice bar and herbal tea store in Chinatown. I decided to give myself a little over an hour for this experience. The day of, I left the office and started on my journey. I was so scared. I had no idea what I was doing, venturing out into a neighborhood on my own. But there was a sense of freedom and joy in it. I had made a breakthrough.

And you know what? I had so much fun. At times, I felt a bit silly. I wandered into a gift shop where the shop owners only spoke Chinese. I realized that I had experienced a little bit of Chinese culture. I had to figure out how to make purchases, ask for directions when I was lost, and read signs written in Chinese. Yes, I found the juice bar. I sat with locals and had some bubble tea. I also purchased some herbal teas.

One of my favorite movies is *My Big Fat Greek Wedding*. Every time I watch this movie, I realize that I had never tried Baklava. Yes, on day seven, I went to Greektown. I went from shop to shop until I found a café infamous for its pastries. I found baklava. There were so many flavors, I asked the server for a recommendation. I sat at the bar, had some coffee, and enjoyed a slice of honey maple flavored baklava. When I returned to the office, I shared my experiences with my colleagues.

Now it's your turn.

Are you ready? Do you live or work near Chinatown, Greektown, or another neighborhood that is rich in culture? Decide which neighborhood you would like to explore for an hour. Plan which shops you would like to visit or cuisines that you would like to experience. It is okay; there will be enough time. Now add this to your calendar. To help you prepare, here are some notes from my journal:

1. Wear light, breathable clothing during summertime.
2. Make sure that you have comfortable walking shoes.
3. Allow some extra traveling time for traffic.
4. Learn to use Google Translator or a similar app.
5. Do your research, know your destination.
6. Use the wide straw for Bubble Tea.
7. Always have some cash on hand.

Storytime: The Carnival Life

Life is so cyclical. It's amazing how the universe works sometimes. As a teenager in the '90s, my sister and I would spend the summers in Southern Illinois with my grandmother.

One year, I decided that I wanted a summer job. The county fair was in town. I walked a half mile down a rocky road to the fairgrounds to inquire about a job. When I arrived at the fairgrounds, I was directed to a campsite to talk to the operations manager. I knocked on the RV door and this burly woman with a raspy voice and a blonde short cut opened the door.

"Good afternoon, ma'am. I was wondering if you need help working one of the booths."

"I don't think so honey. Come back later," she said. The next day, I walked back up to the fairgrounds under the brutal sun. I knocked on the RV door.

"Hi, ma'am. I was here yesterday inquiring about work. Do you know if anyone needs help at one of the booths?"

"You are persistent," the woman said. "Come with me." I followed her to a cotton candy and caramel apple booth. She introduced me to the staff. I was hired on the spot. I had so much fun learning to make taffy apples and cotton candy.

Fast-forward decades later in 2017, now I was in my thirties as a struggling entrepreneur. I really needed a part-time gig. I recalled how much fun I had working at the county fair as a teenager. I found an ad on Craigslist about a family seeking help with a refreshment stand at the McHenry county fair. I interviewed and got the job. The owners liked me so much that they invited me to travel with them across the Midwest to other fairgrounds. They even offered me room and board in their RV.

This RV was luxury style, complete with a flat-screen television, bar, and stainless steel refrigerator. I learned so much about the fairground worker community. Some of the workers camped out in their cars or tents. This forced me to step out of my comfort zone. At this point, I had been camping only once in my life. The job entailed me sleeping on a couch in an RV at night and waking at 5:00a.m. to open the refreshment stand before the fairgrounds opened each day. The owner offered to show me how to run the business!

You got this!!!

Set your goals

Be brave enough to find the life you want
and courageous enough to chase it.

—Madalyn Beck

CHAPTER 3

Hour 2

Adventure 2: Sail Around the World!

A bathing suit may be required for this adventure. Just kidding. I cannot swim, but I love the water. Every morning, I walk past the Chicago River and see the water taxis docked under the Adams Street bridge. For a moment, I could not remember the last time I took a ride up the Chicago River. I researched the times that the taxis departed. The boats departed every hour. So on day five, I decided to leave the office and hop on a water taxi. I decided to take the water taxi to Navy Pier. I had one goal in mind and that was to eat funnel cake. There are no words to describe leaving work to go to an amusement park. It felt like being a kid again!

I did not know how long the ride would take. But it felt good feeling the wind against my skin. I realized that I was breaking routine when I saw the suits walking across the bridges that towered above me. The nine to five was still in motion, and I was sitting on a boat! Chicago is so rich in architecture, so the view from the River was amazing. On day 15, I hopped on a bus and went to the lakefront. I just sat by the lake, enjoyed the sail boats, closed my eyes, and meditated.

Now it's your turn.

To prepare for this journey, you will need to locate the nearest park, river, lake, or beach located near your office. If you will be boarding a boat, check departure times. If possible, pack a lunch and head out on foot to the nearest waterfront. To help you prepare for your journey, here are notes from my journal:

1.   Pack an extra t-shirt or sweatshirt.
2.   Wear comfortable shoes.

3. Hair in a ponytail, if possible, on boat; it's very windy.
4. A bottle of water or wine.
5. Pack a lunch for picnic.

Storytime: A Series of Firsts

After I graduated from Loyola University in Chicago, I felt like I was ready for a change. At the time, I was working in the hospitality industry. I decided that I was ready to leave the state of Illinois. I had not traveled much or lived out of state. The thought of moving away from family and friends was unnerving. But I felt that there was so much that I had not experienced in life. I talked to my grandmother and she said, "Wherever you go, there you will be." I did not know what this meant at the time, but I was ready.

One day I talked to my HR director. I told her that I wanted to transfer to another hotel. At this point, I had two years of tenure and a good performance record. After some deliberation, we decided that San Antonio would be a good idea. The cost of living was lower than some other cities like San Diego. She recommended me for an interview with the general manager. One problem: I had to board an airplane to go for the job interview.

At this point, I had never been on an airplane before. As the plane started to accelerate down the runway, I changed my mind, and I was ready to abort the mission. That plane was going so fast I could not recognize any of the buildings and objects that flew past the window. But it was too late; within seconds, I was soaring about the clouds.

Well, I aced the interview. I was offered a job as a department manager. I packed my bags and moved to Texas. Another problem: I did not know anyone in Texas. Before leaving Chicago, a colleague introduced me to members of her church. Prior to moving to Chicago, she had lived with her husband in San Antonio while he was stationed there. I was grateful for the connection. When I finally settled in, I reached out to a couple of families that became my foster parents. They welcomed me into their home and helped introduce me to members within the community.

Instead of spending the holidays alone, I was invited to dinner with their family. San Antonio was filled with hardworking, kind people. I remember going to the grocery store and the clerk asked, "How did your day go?" I was so shocked but appreciated the sentiment.

This was the first time that there was no snow during Christmas. I did not need a winter coat, hat, or boots. I learned so much from this experience. This move gave me the courage to take more chances in life. You never know where the next adventure in life with take you.

What are your fears?
Jot them down here

Now imagine that you place them in a bottle,
walk to the beach, and toss it out to sea.

Be yourself; everyone else is already taken.

—Oscar Wilde

CHAPTER 4

Hour 3

Adventure 3: Searching for Buried Treasure

Do you like hunting for buried treasures? Okay, this adventure is not about pirates. But how about exploration of the artistic scene? Art inspires me so much! I am so fascinated by the creativity and messages behind various works. I wanted to challenge myself to explore, go on a personal scavenger hunt. I was able to do this and get to know various artists. A few years back, I was driving south on Lakeshore Drive in Chicago and saw a life-sized sign that read, "you are beautiful." I never forgot how I felt when I first saw this sign. It was the coolest thing that I have ever seen.

Fast-forward years later, I did some research to find out who the artist is behind the message. I discovered that the artist is Matthew Hoffman. There are more than thirty-five art installations throughout the Chicagoland area. I researched and found that there was a "you are beautiful" installation in the West Loop.

On day ten, I took off on a lunch break to find it. Unfortunately, the installation was not there, but I decided to join the movement. I purchased fifty "you are beautiful" stickers. My goal is to place fifty stickers in random locations to help spread the positive message! I started by placing stickers on the back of train schedules. You must be a little clever and sneaky where you decide to leave these stickers. But how cool is it to brighten someone's day!

Now it's your turn.

To prepare for this journey, research museums, art installations, exhibits, and murals in your neighborhood. Do you have a favorite museum? Do you have a favorite artist? Break away and immerse yourself in colors, textures, lights, and sounds. Get out the office, take a map, and just head out on foot like a scavenger hunt. To help you prepare for your journey, here are notes from my journal:

1. Check the schedule of events in your local area.
2. Don't give up if you don't find what you are looking for. Keep moving.
3. Make the best of the experience.
4. Join the movement if there is one.
5. Take advantage of free museum days.
6. Don't overwhelm yourself at the museum; focus on experiencing one exhibit.
7. If you like to take pictures, have a good camera in your bag.
8. Have a bus pass handy for public transit.

Storytime: Let's Travel to the City of Bhutan

Okay, let's close our eyes, take a deep breath, board an airplane, and take a trip across the globe to the Himalayans. Imagine floating over beautiful mountains, rivers, and vegetation. Now let's hike across a bridge swinging over one of these rivers to a country called Bhutan.

Bhutan is a beautiful country that is located between India and China. The people of Bhutan live a remarkably simple life. The king of Bhutan, Jigme Khesar Namgyel Wangchuck, enforces strict polices to protect the environment. There is almost no air pollution. It is also one of the safest places to live. There is little to no crime. Bhutan is infamous for being one of the happiest places on earth. What is their secret? The secret is that the king, Jigme Khesar Namgyel Wangchuck, focuses on GNH (gross national happiness), which measures the well-being of the people.

According to the *World Happiness Report* (2019), happiness has been on the decline in the US since 1973. Some of the factors attributed to unhappiness include social isolation, digital media, recession, and unemployment. These factors led to an increase in depression and suicide rates. The activities that attributed to an increase in happiness include sleep, music, spending time outdoors, volunteer work, and social interactions. So we can conclude that if we focus on activities that have a positive impact on our mental health, we can increase our levels of happiness.

We do not focus on GNH in America. So it is critical that we do something about it. How do we increase our levels of happiness if we do not shift the culture? There are several articles that offer suggestions for simple things that you can do to increase your levels happiness. Some of these suggestions include playing in the leaves, writing a letter to a friend, cloud watching, knitting, or solving a jigsaw puzzle. Whether the break is fifteen minutes or one hour, take the time to care for you!

What does living
deliberately
mean to you?

Reflect here

My mission in life is not merely to survive, but to thrive; and to do so with some passion, some compassion, some humor, and some style.

—Maya Angelou

CHAPTER 5

Hour 4

Adventure 4: Swim with the Dolphins!

Clearwater, Florida, is so captivating. The white sandy beaches, clear-blue water, skies that goes on for miles. While on a weekend excursion in Clearwater, I went on a boat tour to see the dolphins. The tour guide pointed out historical sites and celebrity homes.

John Travolta, Tom Cruise, and Hulk Hogan are among some of Hollywood's rich and famous that own property in Tampa. I absolutely loved Clearwater. The town was so laid back. A calmer vibe than the hustle and bustle of Chicago. As we circled the bay, there were schools of dolphins following our boat. They were racing through the waters trying to keep up. It was hilarious watching the dolphins leap into the air, splash, then leap into the air again.

Okay, you may not be able to literally swim with the dolphins. But you can go on an underwater sea adventure! Yes, get out of the office and go touch a starfish or stingray. There are so many cool underwater species to observe like Beluga whales, dolphins, seahorses, giant crabs, jellyfish, and coral reefs!

On day twenty-three, I hopped in an Uber on my lunch break and headed to the aquarium. I purchased a ticket to the 12:30 p.m. aquatics show. I was so excited. It had been years since I had been to the aquarium. I should have allowed more time for travel, but I made it to see the end of the dolphin show! It was so cool seeing the dolphins interact with the trainers. The dolphins are one of the smartest creatures on the planet. I also saw Bella, a baby Beluga whale, and the jellyfish exhibit. The jellyfish are so majestic. Watching them swim is like poetry in motion. There are so many species, various colors, shapes, and sizes. One of my best lunch breaks ever!

Now it's your turn.

Most cities have zoos or aquariums. Add an underwater sea adventure or afternoon safari to your schedule. To help you prepare for your journey, here are notes from my journal:

1. Purchase tickets online if possible.
2. Give yourself extra time for travel.
3. Plan for the exhibit that you want to see.
4. Relax and enjoy yourself.
5. Have a bus pass handy.
6. Plan for inclement weather if outdoors.

Storytime: Waterfalls in the City

Growing up on the West Side of Chicago, I had heard my classmates recap family vacations spent in the Grand Canyon or the magical Niagara Falls. We could not afford to travel, so I lived vicariously through my friends. I knew what a waterfall was. There were images in cartoons and romantic comedies. It was not until I was twelve years old that I realized that Chicago had a lakefront.

I still remember the first time we drove down Lakeshore Drive. Where did all this water come from? Why didn't anybody tell me? The beaches, the boats, people running and planning volleyball in the sand; it kind of felt like Plato's *Allegory of the Cave*. I was living with a limited view of the world.

The summers were brutal in the city. It would get so hot outside that you could fry an egg on the sidewalk; and we did fry eggs on the sidewalk. During the dog days of summer, we cooled off by running through the sprinklers. Some of our neighbors had waddling pools.

But there was nothing like uncapping the fire hydrants. The older kids would unscrew the caps to the hydrants. Next they would place a heavy wooden plank against the opening. This would cause the water to shoot at least ten to twelve feet into the air. We would run with bare feet underneath the cool towering water. The water formed the most magnificent rainbow over the block. If you were afraid to go in, those crazy boys would grab you, cradle you, and carry you in.

We did not care if the street was inaccessible to vehicles; we just had fun. Sometimes a fire engine would pull up and a fireman would put the cap back on. But there were times when the firemen let us play until we grew tired. We danced under those waterfalls until the sun went down.

I still have not been to Niagara Falls, but I wonder if it would compare to the waterfalls on my childhood block.

Shout it out!
How are you feeling
in this moment?

Reflect here

Time is more value than money. You can get more money, but you cannot get more time.

—Jim Rohn

CHAPTER 6

Hour 5

Adventure 5: Get on Up and Dance!

Yes, I walked out of the office and got my dance on! Who says that you cannot dance while on the clock? On day twenty-one, I went to the cultural center and was jamming to the legends of house music. On day eighteen, I went to the Picasso to see a live band, took lunch, and enjoyed the smooth R&B sounds.

I love to dance. I think that I got this from my mother. My mother loved to party and have a good time. Her favorite song was "Friday Night Just Got Paid." There are several free music events and festivals throughout the city, especially during the spring and summer time.

I reviewed the city's calendar of events and discovered that the various orchestras, bands, and chambers have rehearsal sessions that you can attend for free! The word *free* helps when budgeting for eighteen adventures in eighteen days. Some of the chamber rehearsals are held in community centers or on lawns at city parks.

I saw the most beautiful violinist and pianist collaboration at the cultural center. Absolutely amazing! It was a packed house. It only cost me two dollars and twenty-five cents for my bus fare. I was able to sit back, relax, and enjoy a free classical music experience.

Now it's your turn.

Whether you like classical music, jazz, blues, or rock, research venues in your area! Can you break away at lunch and sit in on set? Let your hair down and have a good time. The work will be there when you return to the office. To help you prepare for your journey, here are notes from my journal:

1. Pack lunch.
2. If it's the summer, bring bottled water.

3. Be familiar with the venue location.
4. Get up and dance if moved or appropriate.
5. Take advantage of free concerts and events.

Storytime: Dancing Out of My Shell

In high school, I was extremely shy. But I was extremely smart. The popular kids liked me because I could help them with their homework. The smart kids like me because I was kind of geeky. Instead of taking physical education, I signed up for dance.

To get credit for physical education, we had to attend dance practice after school every day. We were required to learn dance routines and perform in fall, spring, winter and exhibition shows. Our dance team was equivalent to elite sport athletes. Our dance instructor was a professional dancer with the Alvin Alley Dance company in Chicago. She taught us various techniques. We learned jazz, ballet, tap, spiritual, and African dance. We performed routines from different eras, from swing to hip hop.

Our shows were full productions. Behind the curtains, it was pure madness. There were costumes for each dance sequence. There were sound and lighting crews. As the guests entered the auditorium, there were programs that adorned the names of the dancers.

At 7:00 p.m., it was showtime. All the hours of practicing were put to the test. Our dance instructor went on stage to welcome the audience. Next, the lights dimmed, and the music glared. "Let's welcome our Sullivan High School dance team." There was no turning back now. When I was on stage, I was no longer the shy girl. I came out of that shell. Dancing was a way for me to express myself in ways that I thought was impossible.

I recall a fable about a child throwing starfish back into the water that washed up on the beach. Someone asked the child, "Why are you performing such an act? There are thousands of them, you cannot possibly save them all."

The child replied, "But to the one that I saved, it was worth it to him." This is what dance did for me.

What are you grateful for?

Reflect here

Everything in the universe has
rhythm. Everything dances.

—Maya Angelou

CHAPTER 7

Hour 6

Adventure 6: Random Acts of Kindness

The world does not revolve around me! Hard to imagine, but yes, it's true! I learned that I can quickly shift my mood by focusing on others. I was also inspired by the many documentaries that I watched regarding brave souls travelling the world, performing acts of kindness.

I started on my random acts of kindness journey by putting inspirational stickers on the back of train schedules. I was hoping that someone would see the sticker while commuting, and it would bring a smile to his or her face. A couple of times, I purchased gift cards at the local coffee shop and asked the cashier to use it to pay for the next customer's order.

Some days, I would just walk around, and when I encountered a homeless person, I would give him or her the cash that I had on hand. When I get off the train in the morning, I walk past a shoeshine station. I noticed an elderly black man hunched over polishing the shoes of professional men, many in suits and ties. I felt compelled to show the elderly man that he is appreciated. So every day when I approached that shoeshine station, I dropped a tip in the jar. The first time that I did this, the elderly man looked bewildered. But he said, "Thank you," and quickly returned to servicing the customer in the chair. I realized that there are a lot of opportunities to perform random acts of kindness throughout the community during the workday.

I get ideas of random acts of kindness from Facebook groups or other articles online. There is so much content out there. I am working to add one random act of kindness to my schedule daily. Some random acts of kindness may include complimenting someone, taking a friend or colleague to lunch, or just taking the time to listen to someone's story. Shift your day by spending just one hour bringing a smile to someone's face.

Now it's your turn.

Make a list of random acts of kindness that resonate with your spirit. You do not need to spend money. Maybe start by saying "good morning," or "how are you doing today?" To help you prepare for your journey, here are notes from my journal:

1. Research examples of random acts of kindness.
2. Stay motivated by joining a Facebook groups or online communities.
3. Consider serving for one hour in the community.
4. Don't forget to journal every day.

Storytime: Listening to "The Signs"

One day I was the last person to leave the office. After hours, usually around six p.m. or so, the housekeeping crew arrives. I was still sitting in my cubicle, wrapping up for the day. The housekeeper approached my cubicle. I pulled the trash can from under my desk. "Hello," I replied.

She smiled and proceeded to throw away the trash. I heard a whisper, *Give the housekeeper the money that you have in your pocket.* Of course, I was hesitant. But I heard it again, *Give her all of the money that you have.* "All of it," I replied to myself. Well, I only had twelve dollars on hand. I was really trying to stretch that twelve dollars into payday Friday.

I did as a I was instructed to do. I found an envelope and placed the cash inside. I wandered the floor, looking for the kind woman. I found her cleaning the men's restroom. I walked into the men's restroom and handed her the envelope. She looked bewildered. I simply said, "Thank you, this is for you."

Weeks later, she left a thank-you note on my desk. It does not matter if you are the CEO or a member of the janitorial staff. Everyone is important and should be equally loved and valued.

What did you learn about yourself today?

Reflect here

Above all else, be kind.

—Unknown

CHAPTER 8

Hour 7

Adventure 7: Hop on the Trolley!

Oh my goodness! How many times do we watch the trolleys pass us by? Sometimes we wave at the tourists and marvel at how much fun they are having. One of the best adventures was when I walked out of the office and hopped on one of those red trollies. I felt like a rebel. I felt so free! I had so much fun!

On day twenty-seven, I rode the trolley around the loop for an hour. I sat at the top of the trolley so that the wind and sun touched my face. We drove past historical landmarks along the river. I waved at the blue suits that disappeared into the rush hour crowds. There was a comedic tour guide that had us laughing hysterically.

As a Chicagoan, I have some historical knowledge, but there is always something new that I learn during these tours. I had not been on a tour in years! I could have ridden on that trolley all day. This was one of my favorite experiences.

I was probably the only one on the trolley that had to jump off and race back to the office. I was so envious of the tourists that were able to continue to explore. My hair was a mess from the high winds, but I didn't care. Yes, going back to work sucked, but my spirit was lifted for the remainder of the day!

Now it's your turn.

You know you see that trolley. Well, hop on! Take a moment to review the trolley schedule. How long is the tour? Can you hop on and hop off? Where are the boarding locations? Is there a boarding location near your workplace? Here are some notes from my journal to help you prepare for your journey:

1. Arrive early to board.
2. Pack lunch or plan a lunch stop.

3. Bring a bottle of water.
4. Plan where you want to get on and off.
5. Sit on the top of the trolley if weather permits.

Storytime: "The Magic of Life"

In my senior year at Loyola, I dropped out of college. I was exhausted working full-time and going to school full-time. I was so embarrassed that I did not even tell my grandmother. I just withdrew from classes. I was working in retail, but I needed more income to pay for my apartment and other living expenses.

I saw an article in the classifieds for a front desk clerk at a residential building near Belmont Harbor. There was one catch: the hours were third shift, 11:00 p.m.–7:00 a.m. I had never worked third shift before. But the pay was significantly higher than minimum wage. I took the job. In the back of my mind, I knew that I would register for classes the next semester, so I would not be able to work third shift for long.

About a month or so later, I saw that a job fair was being held at a hotel in downtown Chicago. They were hiring for concierges and front desk agents. I decided to attend the event. When I arrived at the ballroom of the hotel, there were hundreds of job seekers. I was standing in a line, studying the interviewers sitting behind the banquet tables screening resumes. I noticed that some attendees were going to the left, and some to the right. Those going to the right were exiting the building.

You could see the disappointment in their faces as they pushed through the glass doors. Those going to the left were escorted to a posh seating area where they were offered some refreshments. *I want to go to the left,* I thought. Before it was my turn to interview, I shifted lanes. Why did I shift lanes? I don't know. But when I finally got to the front of the line, the kind gentleman said, "Hello." I smiled and introduced myself. "I know you," he said. "You are the young lady that works the front desk in the building where I live."

"Yes," I replied.

"Go to the left and take a seat," he said.

What is your favorite adventure so far?

Reflect here

When you give something 100% focus
because your life depends on it
                              —Alex Honnold

CHAPTER 9

Hour 8

Adventure 8: Get a Tattoo

Okay, I have not had a chance to do this one yet. But how cool would it be to get a tattoo on your lunch break? Tattoos are symbolic for living on the edge. Getting a tattoo in the middle of the workday, perfect! There are so many tattoo shops in the city. I was originally thinking that I would get a Henna tattoo. Have you ever seen these? They are intricate and fascinating.

Henna tattoos are used in various religions and cultures. In the Hindu culture and religion, they are painted on the bride to signal joy, beauty, and spiritual awakening. So my Henna tattoo would reflect my "spiritual awakening." I have always wanted to get a tattoo. But like other fellow trypanophobia's, I am terrified.

Of course, some of my friends have them. My ex-boyfriend has a tattoo of a Bible scripture on his forearm. But that's a story for another day. I have asked the brave tattooed ones: "will it hurt?" and have received mixed reviews. It sounds like it depends on the location of the tattoo. For example, the ankle may be more sensitive than the belly area.

Enough of the overthinking. I did some research and found a tattoo shop close to work. I made an appointment to check out some temporary tattoo options. I also located some mobile Henna artists in the area.

Now it's your turn.

Research tattoo artists and shops in your area. What will a tattoo symbolize to you? Is there a friend, family member, or life event that you would like to capture? Maybe a symbol of you living a more deliberate life. Here are some notes from my journal to help you prepare for your journey:

1. It may help to research the symbol or image that you want.
2. It's ok to go for a consultation before the you decide.
3. Make sure that you are comfortable with your artist.
4. Block time off your calendar and indulge in body art.

Storytime: Minimalism

On my quest to live more deliberately, I found out about a movement called *minimalism*. I had no clue what *minimalism* was. I watched a documentary, and I was hooked. I realized that I have been a minimalist my entire life.

I have always dreaded figuring out what to wear in the morning. Getting dressed is my least favorite activity. I also hate going shopping. At first I thought that I had a social phobia or something. But I realized that I don't enjoy spending time wandering around the mall. I think it has to do with my fear of time. I have always felt that time is running out. So shopping is no fun for me because it takes too many hours from my timeline.

I used the principles of minimalism to simplify my life. I started by donating clothes, shoes, and other items around the house that I don't use. I reduced the clutter in the house so that it took me less time to find things, fewer items to clean. I stopped spending money on items that I do not need. When I reduced the stuff in my life, I gained more time to focus on more important things in life.

The biggest revelation to me was that I stopped caring so much about what people think. I get dressed in the morning, comb my hair, and head out the door. I am no longer concerned about the latest fashions, and I stopped comparing myself to others. Minimalism has forced me to love me. I have had such a liberating experience.

Today, share your experiences with someone

Reflect here

When you realize that this life is
yours, everything changes.

—A. J. Leon

CHAPTER 10

Hour 9

Adventure 9: Go to the Movies! Yes, Now!

Yes, I went to the movies. On day fourteen, I broke the rules of engagement. Why not? I did not realize how excited I was until I arrived at the theater. Earlier in the week, I saw the previews for a movie about a young professional that worked his way up corporate ladder to an upper-management level position. In the previews, the young professional struggled with the everyday monotony of the corporate workplace.

The movie addresses the double life that we all lead. When we are in the workplace, we conform to a certain set of rules. Some of these rules may or may not align with who we are. And sometimes we can experience cognitive dissonance. I could relate to the main character in the movie. I checked the running time and discovered that the run time was a little over an hour.

I hopped in an Uber at 11:45 a.m. and made it just in time for the noon showing. I grabbed some popcorn and Reese's pieces. I sat back in the chair and enjoyed the show. When the lights went down and the previews started, I said to myself, *You are actually going to do this.*

The movie was hilarious. I had a great time. I left the show at 1:30 p.m. and returned to work. My colleague asked me what happened.

"I went to the movies," I said.

"You actually went to the movies on your lunch break?" she replied.

"Yes, I did," I replied. I had the biggest smile on my face.

Now it's your turn.

Check out the new movie releases! There may also be some independent film festivals or other film events that you are interested in attending. Pick a showtime between 11:00 a.m.–3:00 p.m. Block at least an hour and a half to two hours off your calendar. Now go! Here are some notes from my journal to help you prepare for your journey:

1. Attend the 11:00 a.m. show if possible.
2. Plan for thirty minutes of movie trailers
3. You may or may not get to finish the show, but that's okay.
4. Don't forget the popcorn and your favorite snacks.
5. Sit back and relax.

Storytime: Free Solo

Have you heard of "free solo climbing"? This is a sport where skilled athletes climb rocks without equipment or harnesses. There is literally no apparatus to protect them from falling. It is a life or death situation.

Some of the rocks conquered are El Capitan in Yosemite National Park. El Capitan is three thousand feet of pure granite rock. Free soloists are so brave and fearless. Climbing without ropes means that they must depend on themselves. This is a different level of accomplishment or achievement for these athletes. They must overcome their fear and cheat death.

I don't think that I have the courage to free solo, but I climbed one of the tallest buildings in Chicago: the John Hancock Center. The John Hancock Center towers ninety-six stories above the city of the Chicago. Every year, there is a race to climb the stairs to the top of the building.

One year, I decided to register for the event. After four months of training, I was ready for the event. Once I entered the stairwell, I freaked out. How was I going to climb ninety-six floors? I am no athlete. After crawling up a couple of flights of stairs, I almost gave up. *You can do this*, I said to myself.

It was extremely warm in the stairwell. I continued to climb. I paced myself. I tried not to pay attention to the numbers on the walls reminding me that I was stories from the finish line. You know what? I finished the climb in forty-five minutes. It is amazing what you can do when you put your mind to it.

Take someone with you today
How did it go?

Reflect here

It's not enough to be born free;
I must live my freedom!
—Esther M. Friesner

CHAPTER 11

Hour 10

Adventure 10: Grow

I grew up on the West Side of Chicago. I did not know this when I was younger, but our neighborhood was in the middle of a food desert. Food deserts is a systemic problem in America. Millions of Americans do not have access to fresh fruits or vegetables. This is primarily due to the lack of grocery stores in impoverished neighborhoods. For those that may have access to fresh foods, they cannot afford it. Someday I want to get involved in the development of a community garden within my old neighborhood.

After some research, I discovered that there are several nonprofit organizations that are sponsoring these gardens. On day twenty, I decided to visit a community garden out of curiosity just to see one up close and personal. I was also hoping to gather some information regarding volunteer opportunities.

The community garden that I decided to visit was in the West Loop, about a five-minute cab ride. At 11:45 a.m., I hopped in a cab and headed to the community garden site. I was so excited when I arrived. It was the first community garden that I have ever visited.

The garden was positioned alongside of a commercial building in a repurposed vacant lot. There was a gate with the word "grow" in multicolor marker on a poster board. I saw wheelbarrows filled with soil and rows of vegetables sprouting out from the ground. There were also some unpotted plants scattered about. The gate to the garden was locked, and there were no volunteers onsite. I found it ironic but profound to see a beautiful garden in the middle of a concrete jungle. I almost cried at the site of the garden. I want to learn as much as possible so that I can volunteer and advocate for healthier communities.

Now it's your turn.

Do you have a green thumb? There are several community gardens and greenhouses that could use your help. Get out of the office and grow something! Here are some notes from my journal to help you prepare for your journey:

1. Research garden locations and hours.
2. Pack lunch if one is not provided.
3. Stay hydrated, bring a couple of bottles of water.
4. Wear long sleeves and long pants.
5. Wear boots if working garden.

Storytime: Road Trip to Southern Illinois

Every summer, my grandmother would take us on a five-hour road trip to Southern Illinois. The Land of Lincoln is a beautiful green flatland. We would pile into the 1970 Lincoln at about 5:00 a.m. and head south on I-57. Once we cleared the city, the scenery changed— no high rises, no buses, or cabs. We drove past fields of wheat, grain, and corn. The corn stalks towered more than four feet into the air. There were rows of the yellow crop as far as the eyes could see. My sister and I were mesmerized by the farmlands covered with grazing cows and horses. In the city, our only experience with animals is at the zoo behind enclosures.

Our family in Southern Illinois grew fresh fruits and vegetables. The family owns a plot of land the size of a small baseball field. My grandmother and grandfather would wake at 4:00 a.m., eat breakfast, and work all day in the garden, tending to the crops. The garden was filled with colorful rows of corn, watermelon, cantaloupe, peas, greens, cabbage, tomatoes, cucumbers, and okra.

My grandmother would take us into the garden to help collect bushels to share with the neighbors. We always had fresh fruits and vegetables on the table while visiting my grandparents in Southern Illinois—from the garden to the table. I was not a fan of fried okra but loved fried green tomatoes.

My grandmother knew how to survive off the land. She would go fishing from sunrise to sunset. Sometimes we would grab a pole and join her on the banks of Mississippi. She taught us how to put a live worm on a hook. This is not my favorite task when fishing, but I can do it. I was so proud of myself when I caught my first fish. I am grateful for the summers spent in Southern Illinois with my grandmother.

How can you integrate principles of Ikigai into your lifestyle?

Reflect here

I believe that the very purpose of life is to be happy. From the very core of our being, we desire contentment.

—Dalai Lama

CHAPTER 12

Hour 11

Adventure 11: Make a Wish

On day twenty-seven, I visited the biggest fountain in Chicago, Buckingham Fountain. I brought lunch with me so that I can sit and enjoy the spectacular water show. Mermaids, seahorses, three layers of architecture, water cascading 150 feet into the air against the backdrop of the lakefront. This was an emotional day as I was approaching the end of the experiment. I recorded video footage of my visit; you can visibly see the rollercoaster of emotions that I was experiencing in that moment.

Anyway, I believe in the power of wishes. So I walked up to the fountain, took a deep breath, threw a quarter in, and made a wish. I can't share what the wish was; it's a secret.

On another day, I visited the Poetry Foundation. Have you ever heard of a wish tree? I had never actually seen one until this day. Well as I walked through the garden, I noticed that there were white tags with messages of hope for the world hanging from the branches of trees. I was so inspired by the site of the white sea of love surrounding me. I read some of the messages: "I pray for peace in the world," "I wish that children have a safe place." So I grabbed a blank tag from the patio table and scribbled: "My wish is global health and happiness."

I researched the history of wish trees and found out that they can be traced back to the early 1700s. In many cultures, the natives believe that these trees are connected to divine energy, light, and spirit beings. This divine energy brings healing, prosperity, or grants wishes. Some of these trees are filled with lucky coins or other keepsakes.

Now it's your turn.

What are your wishes? Take a break, find a way to release your wish to the universe. Preferably a peaceful setting so that you can reflect, meditate, and harness your energy and light. Here are some notes from my journal to help you prepare for your journey:

1. Pack lunch.
2. Plan for inclement weather.
3. Write your wishes down in your journal.
4. If you are visiting a wishing tree, bring a pen and lucky trinket to donate to the tree.

Storytime: Leprechauns and Lucky Charms

I must tell you about my maroon lucky jacket. If you believe in lucky charms, my jacket would be a one of them. In my twenties, this jacket took me a lot of places and helped open doors. I wore this jacket on all my job interviews. I was unstoppable with my lucky jacket on. I think that my grandmother purchased this for me at Sears or Goldblatt's. When she purchased this jacket, it was part of a two-piece suit and came with a skirt. Initially, I wore this suit primarily to church. But when I moved out, I wore the jacket to job interviews and other social events.

The jacket was double breasted with two rolls of gold buttons down the front. The shape of the jacket was military style, and the length fell right at my knees. I felt good in this jacket. It was professional and very flattering to my figure. This jacket helped me open and share more about myself. The first job offer that I received was at a mall in downtown Chicago. The second offer: concierge at a hotel in downtown Chicago. See, it was magical!

I don't know about the existence of leprechauns. My cousin saw a little green leprechaun when he was seven years old. A child that young could not possibly make something like this up, right? The thought of a pot of gold at the end of a rainbow sounds mythical. But I do know that lucky charms exist. My girlfriend reminded me of the ritual when it was time to throw away that lucky jacket. I wish I held onto that jacket. I could use some of that good luck today.

Quick Check in.

How are you doing?

Reflect here

Only those who will risk going too far can
possibly find out how far one can go.

—T. S. Eliot

CHAPTER 13

Hour 12

Adventure 12: Create, Make, Innovate

Yes, I worked on an arts and crafts project where I had to build something with my hands. I stepped out of my comfort zone and prepared for my first public art show. Have you heard of a busy board? Well, I came up with the bright idea to create one for adults. I had to go to Home Depot and buy pieces of wood, a drill, a jigsaw, and other gadgets. What the heck is a jigsaw?

I watched some YouTube videos for tips to learn how to make this board. I then made a list of items needed for the project! I was so uncomfortable. I did not know what questions to ask the patient Home Depot associates. The look on their faces when I struggled to describe what I was trying to do, priceless. They looked at me like: "Lady, you have no clue what you are doing, do you?"

It took me hours to complete the project. I had to learn how to use power tools. I had to master how to not split wood while drilling a screw. There were a lot of mistakes along the way. I had to throw prototypes away and start over dozens of times. I was so frustrated that I almost gave up. Splinters hurt. I broke my fingernails! But you know what? I did it. I finished the piece. My art was displayed for months in a gallery for hundreds of patrons to enjoy. I was so proud of myself.

I also attended a couple of paint-and-sip parties. I do not know how to draw, but wine was involved, so I decided to give it a try! I did not do that badly! With a little assistance, the painting looked similar the original that we were replicating. Allowing myself to experiment has inspired me to be more creative!

Now it's your turn.

There are a lot of workshops where you can sharpen your wood making, candle making, painting, quilting, or other crafting skills.

Get out of the office and make something! Tell the boss that you are going to make something! Here are some tips from my journal to help you prepare for your journey:

1. Research workshops at libraries, schools, museums, etc.
2. Purchase the materials needed if not provided.
3. Plan your nine to five around the project schedule.
4. If you need inspiration, watch YouTube videos.
5. Don't give up!

Storytime: The Shark Tank

In 2013, I auditioned for the show *The Shark Tank*. *The Shark Tank* production crew came to Chicago's Shedd Aquarium. Hundreds of entrepreneurs were given the opportunity to pitch their ideas. A friend and I decided to audition.

It was a mild sunny day along Chicago's lakefront. The production crew was set to interview the first five-hundred entrepreneurs that showed up that day. We met up at 9:00 a.m. that day in Grant Park to guarantee a spot. There were already over one hundred entrepreneurs in line. Some had spent the night camped in the park. We were numbers 200 and 201. I was so excited to be a part of the experience.

We waited in that line for almost three hours. By noon, they started handing out wristbands, passing out waivers for us to review, sign, etc. My idea was a privacy screen for vehicles. I purchased fabric from the store and sewed a prototype by hand. I also prepared a presentation. I was so nervous.

After more than four hours of waiting outside, we finally made it into the Shedd Aquarium. We were guided to a conference room where we had two minutes to pitch our idea. My colleague had a table next to mine. I noticed that there were some entrepreneurs that were directed to a video room to record their stories after they pitched. When it was my turn, my voice started shaking. I talked way too fast. Well, we did not make it to the next step in the process. I was so disappointed. I never heard back. But I am so grateful for the experience and that I have the story to share.

What do you need to let go of?

Jot it down here

I did then what I knew how to do. Now
that I know better, I do better.

—Maya Angelou

CHAPTER 14

Hour 13

Adventure 13: Live Like a Celebrity!

On day nine, I visited the set of *Saturday Night Live*! When I arrived, I posed for photos on the red carpet, Hollywood style. I felt like a movie star! I walked down the long red carpet, took the elevators up to the legendary studio 8H.

When I stepped off the elevator, it was a little dark. I was like, *Okay, what did I get myself into?* I opened the double doors and walked down the red carpet. As I took a deep breath, the television screens illuminated, there were spotlights, music, the doors opened, and I heard: "Welcome, it's Saturday Night!" I was transported to the production set.

The set was filled with costumes worn by legendary cast members like Eddie Murphy, Rachel Dratch, Dan Aykroyd, Tina Frey, Whitney Brown, and John Belushi. There were artifacts from the dressing rooms! I sat on the Wayne's World couch! I was a contestant on the Jeopardy Show! One of the coolest parts was sitting at the table where the cast members read the scripts. The simulated control room was surreal! I was immersed in stage props, prosthetics, sketches, scenic sets, and highlight reels. The exhibit was so awesome!

Did you know that the *Saturday Night Live Show* has been on the air for more than forty years? I recall hearing the skits in the background as a child. I remember my parents telling me to go to bed by 9:00 p.m., too early to view risky programs. It was like a rite of passage when I became old enough to stay up and watch late-night television.

Now it's your turn.

Look for a broadcast museum, talk show, or other production set exhibits in your area. Become a celebrity for an hour! Here are some tips from my journal to help you prepare for your journey:

1. Look for your favorite character costumes.
2. Allow a little over an hour to experience it fully.
3. Purchase tickets online if possible.
4. Don't forget your diamond-studded celebrity shades.

Storytime: Rap Contest

It was the summer of 1989, the end of a formative decade of fashion, music, and culture. The eighties had a lasting impact on our generation. This was the decade that brought us Michael Jackson's "Thriller." The guys dressed like the king of pop. The red-and-black jacket, high pants, glitter socks, and infamous glove. The girls wore scrunchies and big ponytails like Madonna. This was the end of an era of boom boxes and break dancing on cardboard boxes in the streets. The streets were filled with the sounds of Run DMC, the Beastie Boys, and Rob Base. New Kids on the Block's videos played on repeat on MTV. George Bush SR was the president, and the nation was preparing for the Gulf War.

These were the days when it was safe to play outside all day. Neighbors left their front doors open so that we could stop by and grab a glass of Kool-Aid on a warm summer day. I remember playing hide-and-seek until the wee hours of the night. Block club parties transformed the neighborhoods into one big family reunion. All the neighbors brought their barbecue grills and coolers out into the streets. The 1980s was a decade of community, togetherness.

We had recently moved to the north side to live with my grandmother. I was in the eighth grade. Our school announced that a local radio station was partnering with the Chicago Lung Association to host a rap contest. To enter the contest, you had to record a rap about the dangers of smoking. The teachers asked if anyone would like to participate. I thought to myself, *I do not know how to rap or rhyme. But I know how to write. Okay, let us do it!* First, I wrote the lyrics. Next, I had to figure out how to use my grandmother's boom box to record voice-over music. I stuttered several times, rewrote some of the lyrics until I got it right. Once I had the demo recorded, I submitted the tape to the judges. After submission of the demo, months went by. We did not hear anything from the Chicago Lung Association. In the winter of 1989, they announced the winning schools. Guess what? I won third place. Our school was recognized publicly on the radio and on billboards and posters across the city of Chicago. It is amazing what can happen in life when you have the courage to seize the moment. Enjoy these lyrics from the demo.

Do you want to know what's in and what is out?
Smokin' is what this rap's about. I'm on the mic to let you know.
That smokin' is not the way to go. Our world was meant for love and care. Not to have smoke polluting that air. We are losing more people every day, month, year. So don't be influenced by you peers. If you want to know what's good for heart and lungs, don't slip a cigarette on your tongue.
I'm ending this rap to let you know, that smokin' is not the way to go.

How many hours of your life

have you re-captured so far?

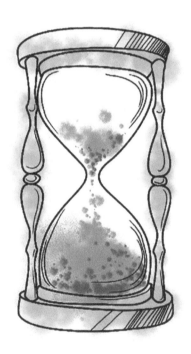

Reflect here

All life is an experiment. The more experiments you make the better.
—Ralph Waldo Emerson

CHAPTER 15

Hour 14

Adventure 14: Play Like a Child

Sometimes you just got to take time away from being an adult! Why not? On day thirty, I attended the "Happy Place" pop-up exhibit. This was a bright interactive exhibit. There were thirteen different rooms filled with sensory experiences formulated to make you smile! There is a bin filled with balls that you can jump into and swim. My favorite part was this room filled with confetti that blows in the air around you. There are buckets of confetti; you reach down, grab, and throw it into the air. Okay, I think that I played in the confetti a couple of times before I left.

On another day, I took the water taxi to Navy Pier. I wanted to go to the carnival in the middle of the day. My mission was to ride the Ferris wheel and get funnel cake. Imagine planning a workday around getting on the Ferris wheel. I did not get a chance to ride the Ferris wheel, but I ate a lot of funnel cake before returning to the office.

I often think about the activities that I enjoyed as a child. What happened to climbing trees, jumping rope, playing hopscotch, making snow angels, or playing hide and seek? Now that I think about it, I don't even play board games anymore. Why don't we play anymore? Let's change that today.

Now it's your turn.

Go jump on a trampoline, play at the park. Yes, sit on a swing! Go on the slide! The latest trend are these pop-up exhibits. Don't be afraid to be silly. Here are some notes from my journal to help you prepare for your journey:

1. Try to take an early lunch to prevent long waits.
2. Pack lunch if you are going to the park.
3. What season is it? Do you need to do something indoors?
4. Take an extra outfit if activity is involved.

Storytime: Letter to Myself, Five Years from Now

This is a letter to me to be read in five years. When I read this letter in five years, I would have lived a more deliberate life. I would have loved more than the day before. I have learned to trust and open my world a bit more. This is going to take some courage, but hopefully I would have made another lifetime friend.

I love myself more. I have learned to be kind to others because true happiness is found in taking care of others. I have transitioned to a new career; it is so awesome. I am doing what I love. By this time, I will be a published author and blogger. I am using my platform to help others on the path to health and wellness.

Hopefully, I will have a passport and would have at least traveled to another continent. I'm thinking that somewhere in Europe would be ideal. I have heard stories of the mesmerizing green countryside in Ireland, and I also saw Michael Jordan stand in front of the Leaning Tower of Pisa in Paris. Paris sounds romantic; I think that I may go there.

I will not be so isolated from the world. Living life in a bubble is not living at all. I will allow others to go along on my journeys. I will talk less and listen more. I learn so much from just listening to what other humans have experienced. My inspiration comes from observing others. I would also like to continue to inspire others. I want my life, creativity, and light to inspire others. I want to be continuing to be brave, fearless, and powerful. Live as an example for others. More importantly, I will make sure that I am more connected to nature and the universe. I will take the time to appreciate nature and thank her for the oxygen, water, sun, and the wind. Five years from now, I would have achieved all these things and have presented a better version of myself to the world.

Draft a letter to your future self.
What would it say?

Jot down some thoughts here

Thank you for being you in a world
full of somebody else's.

—Mark Anthony

CHAPTER 16

Hour 15

Adventure 15: Explore hidden caves

I am intrigued by the fact that there is a city beneath our city. Apparently, construction started in 1951. I had heard stories of the Pedway being a way for gangsters to move through the city inconspicuously. Of course, it was also a way to avoid the lake effect winds.

On day six, I decided to explore the city beneath. The pedway connects some of the city's most iconic landmarks. It's like walking through a maze with surprises around every corner. I probably should have better planned, but I decided to wing it. After some research, I saw that the cultural center had an entrance into the Pedway.

I had a preview of the Pedway years ago after accidently stumbling into it from the lower level of Macy's. There was this eerie feeling like I was wandering into unchartered territory. It was kind of damp, dark, and void of life at certain points. I remember seeing a gypsy woman dressed in elaborate colorful fabrics, covered in jewelry, and playing a tambourine. She was seeking small donations for her musical talents.

As the lunch hour approached, I dashed towards the elevator. The cab driver dropped me on the Washington Street side of the building. I asked the desk attendant how I could enter the Pedway. The attendant pulled out a map and informed me that there was an elevator on the Randolph Street side of the building. I am not good at reading maps, but I nodded like I understood his directions. "Thank you," I said to the attendant.

As I entered the elevator, I grew intense. I had no clue where I was going. The thought of exploring tunnels beneath the earth started to freak me out a bit. As the elevator door opened to the lower, lower, lower level, I carefully stepped out. I did not see any shops underneath the cultural center but followed the tunnel headed west.

I almost turned around, fearing that I might get lost. I continued walking and started to see familiar shops like Macy's. To my surprise, there was art in the Pedway. So cool. I saw mosaic and Tiffany Stained windows installed along the walls of the corridors.

As I continued, I discovered hidden bookstores, diners, and coffee shops. I saw people walking hastily to their destinations. I approached a busy area where the Redline, Blue Line, Orange, and other trains intersected. I hit a dead end. I could not go any further at this point.

I knew exactly where I was. My favorite chocolatier is in this building. I entered the mall and took the elevator up. After selecting my favorite six pieces of chocolate, I decided to head back to work to finish the day. I walked a few blocks down State Street and hopped on the Adams Street bus.

As we passed the pedestrians, crazy cab drivers, and skyscrapers, I took a moment to breathe and enjoy the view. As we crossed the Chicago River, I was shaken by a feeling of internal peace, joy, and happiness.

Now it's your turn.

Is there a hidden cave or forbidden area within your city that you have not had a chance to explore? It may sound a bit scary, but now is the time. You may find some hidden gems and have a unique experience. Here are some notes from my journal to help you prepare for your journey:

1. Take a Pedway map or city map.
2. Plan your route; make sure you are safe.
3. If you don't take lunch, dine at a new spot.

Storytime: Conquering the Direction of the Wind

I had taken some time off from the corporate world to start my own business. A few months passed; it had been a while since I traveled into the city during rush hour mayhem. One day, I had to hop on the train to travel into the city for a coffee meetup. It is a forty-five-minute ride from where I live in the Western Suburbs to the center of the city.

As the train pulled into the station, I could feel the energy of the city, the hustle and bustle. I felt overwhelmed; butterflies filled my stomach. I realized that the few months that I spent away from the city desensitized me a bit.

When I stepped off the train, I was swept up by a crowd of people rushing to conquer the concrete jungle. I realized that I was walking in the wrong direction and pushed against the crowd to navigate to the correct exit.

I looked back over my shoulder and realized that I had unconsciously conquered the wind. I was the only one walking in the direction of the wind. I felt like I had entered another dimension. A dimension where, in that moment, I was making a statement, challenging everything that I was taught, everything I believed. In that moment, I was not on a path that led me to nowhere. This was a pivotal moment for me. In that moment, I realized that is what life is about. How could I create more moments like this in life? Moments where I am in sync with the direction of the wind.

What is your favorite

childhood memory?

Reflect here

Yesterday is gone. Tomorrow has not yet come.
We have only today. Let us begin.
—Mother Teresa

CHAPTER 17

Hour 16

Adventure 16: Poetry, Storytelling, and Book Clubs

As a child, I really enjoyed reading poetry. Some of my favorites included Gwendolyn Brooks, Maya Angelou, and Langston Hughes. I dabbled in writing poetry and short stories in high school. In fact, I wrote two poems that were later published in our senior school newspaper, won a rap contest, and wrote a short story where I captured first place. I have not written in years, so I decided to look for opportunities to attend poetry readings and storytelling events. I discovered that there is a Poetry Foundation in Chicago.

On day twelve, I decided to visit. When I arrived at the Poetry Foundation, I was overwhelmed by the architecture. The library is two stories high with a beautiful garden. There are hundreds of works available within the library. Every poet that you can think of is represented here—from Walt Whitman to Emily Dickinson. I signed up to receive an inspirational email daily. This exposes me to poets that I have never heard of.

One poem that I have fallen in love with is called "A Center" from *A Distant Center* by Ha Jin. "You must hold your distant center. / Don't move even if the earth and heaven quake." After looking around, I found out that there was a monthly lunch book club. Perfect! I attended a couple of book clubs where I met the actual artists. On my way out one day, the receptionist told me about an interactive travelling exhibit where you can write messages for your deceased loved ones. I was not prepared emotionally for this. I sat down in the garden of the library and wrote messages to my mother and grandmother. It is so interesting where these adventures are taking me.

Now it's your turn.

Do you enjoy writing? Is there a novel that you are working on? Are you a photographer? Do you need inspiration for your next project? Visit a poetry, photography, library, or other foundations in your area. You will learn more about event opportunities and gain insight from communities that inspire you. Here are notes from my journal to help you prepare for your journey.

1. Take lunch to eat in the garden.
2. Pay attention to the architecture.
3. Be emotionally prepared for anything.
4. Make a list of favorite poets.
5. Take a journal if you are inspired to write.
6. Look for opportunities to get involved.

Storytime: Activation of Gifts

My best friend told me that I am a good writer. Honestly, I have never thought of myself as a writer. While sorting through some old records from high school, I found a copy of the senior newsletter. In the newsletter, there were stories of academic achievements, What are you going to do next? Some classmates reported that they were off to college. Other students reported that they were going directly to work. It is so interesting how you can spend time with people every day for four years and then never see or hear from them again.

While reading the newsletter, I noticed that there were two poems at the bottom of page 5. I had written two poems of encouragement for our senior class. I had totally forgotten about this. The poems were good enough to be published. In grade school and high school, I had written some short poems and stories.

In the sixth grade, I wrote a ghost story with illustrations. I received recognition for this short story. Decades later, in this moment, I am realizing that I may have a gift. It is time that we all sit down and do an assessment of gifts that we may not know that we possess. What gifts do you possess? Write them down. Activate them now.

Believe
Believe in yourself
Know that you can succeed
Don't give up
Believe
Push for success
Gain the knowledge
Walk with your head held high

Believe
No avenue undiscovered
Believe
There's a lot to learn
There's a lot to know
There's a lot to understand
Believe
If you know in your heart
That you are strong
There's nothing you can't do
Believe
(Teri McElrath's message to senior class, 1994)

Today, do an assessment of
your gifts.

What gifts can you activate?

Reflect here

You can never cross the ocean until you have
the courage to lose sight of the shore
—André Gide

CHAPTER 18

Hour 17

Adventure 17: Spirituality, Meditation, Mindfulness

I was raised in both Christian and Baptist households. My grandmother taught me prayers that I still recite to this day. Although I believe in a higher power, I do not currently identify with a religion. I have always been drawn to the principles of Buddhism.

In Christianity, we are taught to not worship idols or other gods, so the thought of visiting a temple was uncomfortable for me. I researched Buddhist temples near the office. There was a temple nearby that offered the opportunity to learn about the principles without committing to the religion. Buddhism has principles that I am drawn to such as remaining in the moment, being still, and unnecessary suffering.

I am at a point in my life where I need to trust myself, forgive myself, and find true happiness. So I was willing to explore to see if this was for me. I saw that there was a community hour for all walks of life to sit and meditate. I decided to just show up and sit. I was a little nervous because I did not quite know how to meditate.

When I arrived at the Buddhist Temple, I was greeted by one of the volunteers that offered instructions. She assured me that I did not have to be a Buddhist to sit. There were only two of us for the afternoon sitting on this day.

It was quiet at the temple. There was a handsome gentleman who revealed that he was Jewish to me. The volunteer instructed us to take off our shoes. We followed her to a set of double doors where we crossed the threshold into the worship area. The room was a filled with bluish, purplish cushions on the floor and chairs in the back of the room all aligned in perfect rows.

At the front of the room was an altar with a statue of Buddha and pictures of the temple's teachers. I tried not to look at the altar. I glanced at the floor. The volunteer was very patient with me. She taught me how to select the right cushion for my height. She also demonstrated various positions that are comfortable for sitting. After the instructions, she hit this large gong. My body vibrated from the deafening sound. Everything in the room grew silent. I tried to focus on my breath instead of the lengthy to-do list in my head, or the sounds of the vehicles passing by.

After the session, my shoulders felt lighter, my head clear. I felt so much better. Like I left everything negative in the room that day!

Now it's your turn.

Okay. If you are into spirituality and religion, plan to visit a church or other sacred area. If this is not for you, maybe find a quiet place where you can practice mindfulness or meditation. Here are notes from my journal to help you prepare for your journey:

1. Pedicure needed for bare feet.
2. Wear comfortable clothing for sitting.
3. Change positions if you need to while sitting.
4. Learn the art of sitting before you attend a session.
5. Decide what you want to let go of.
6. Be present in the moment.

Storytime: Angels Among Us

My grandmother was very spiritual. As children, she taught us various prayers of protection. I still remember what she taught me. My grandmother shared various stories of moments when she knew that she was in the presence of angels. There was a story that she shared that stands out the most.

One evening, she was walking home from work after completing a long shift at a local hospital. It was dark outside; she did not feel safe. During this time, the family lived in the projects of Chicago, and the crime rate was extremely high. There were reports of women being attacked within the common areas of the residences.

My grandmother carefully entered the lobby of the residence that evening. She waited anxiously for the elevator door to open. As the elevator door opened, she quickly stepped inside. As she stepped inside, a gentleman over six feet tall followed closely behind. My grandmother had never seen this gentleman before. They exchanged greetings.

My grandmother noticed that there was an unexplained light that illuminated from the strangers' head. She shared with the stranger how she was frightened due to the reports of women being attacked. The nice stranger offered to escort my grandmother to make sure that she made it to her apartment safely. Angels here on earth?

Breathe
Take a moment

Meditate for 5 minutes

Reflect here

Do not go where the path may lead, go instead
where there is no path and leave a trail.
—Ralph Waldo Emerson

CHAPTER 19

Hour 18

Adventure 18: It's Up to You!

Congratulations! You have recaptured seventeen hours. You have created seventeen moments. This is the most emotional part of the experiment; the end of the journey. The final adventure is your choice. How are you feeling? Was it all worth it? You probably have some good stories to share. Make sure that you capture all your feelings, emotions, and reactions in your journal. I will let you take it from here. You got this!

Hopefully you were inspired by this book and gathered some ideas. Use this book as your journal and record of the day that you changed your life and took control of the clock.

Storytime: Walking Away from It All

I was always healthy and vibrant. Of course, during college, I gained a few pounds eating junk food during late-night study sessions—pizza, ribs, ramen noodles. But I was always able to bounce back and get into shape.

During my four years in college, I worked full-time and attended college full-time. I finished college, but it went so fast I don't recall much. I was working so much. No time for partying. I had decided that I was going to work my butt off to climb the corporate ladder. Well, this led to working sixty to seventy hours per week with little to no sleep.

I wanted to prove that I was smart enough, good enough—just enough. Well, by the time I made it to my late twenties, I burned out. I started to experience a myriad of health issues. These health issues ranged from excessive weight gain and loss to digestive issues, brain fog, lethargy, and a host of other issues.

My health continued to spiral out of control. I went through a period where I had excessive acne, fatigue, anxiety. I visited multiple specialists, including neurologists. I was tested for everything, no diagnosis. My arms were bruised from all the pricks from needles.

This was one of the most frightening times of my life. I remember asking my general practitioner if I was dying. The frustrating part was that there was no diagnosis. I had all these ailments but did not know what was triggering them. The straw that broke the camel's back, as my grandmother would say, was when I had surgery to remove masses in my stomach.

After the surgery, I decided to leave Corporate America and take my chances. I had little money saved, but I knew that I would die from stress if I did not walk away. I needed a break to heal.

Today I am feeling better in my forties than I did in my late twenties. I see the world so much clearer, brighter. I want to spend my life doing what I love, not what I thought that I had to do. I feel like I have been given a second life. I want to live my best life and help others that may be having the same experiences. I am living proof that you can die before death and be born again.

Congratulations! You did it.
What did you learn
about you??

Reflect here

At some point I had to do
what was best for me.

—Teri McElrath

CHAPTER 20

Tips and Next Steps

Tip 1: How to Budget for Your Adventures

I calculated how much it cost for me to go on thirty adventures in thirty days! I calculated that it cost me a total of about $400 or $13 per day. I know that this sounds like a bit much, but consider that I really did not know what I was doing. Now that I know what I want to experience, I can trim the budget a bit.

Budget is critical when planning your ventures out of the office. I quickly realized that being an adventurer, getting out and seeing the world, can be costly. When I first started the personal experiment, I did not set a budget. Halfway through the experiment, the dollars started to add up. I commute to work, so I already had daily travel expenses. I quickly realized that I needed to decide which experiences were more valuable.

Most of the adventures cost between $0 and $40. Examples of events that cost $0 dollars: walks along the lake front, music in the park. Examples of events that may cost more, from $1 to $40: exclusive museum exhibits, pop-up events.

Sitting down and putting together a schedule helped me decide what additional dollars to put aside that week. What helped me reduce costs was taking advantage of free events. I conducted a Google search for free events in the city. There were several festivals, farmers' markets, art events, and literature fests that were free to the public. Well, at least free to browse.

I strategically switched paid events for free events. I also discovered that there are free or discounted days at local museums. I adjusted the schedule accordingly to take advantage of these opportunities. This helped trim the budget significantly.

After making a list of what you would like to experience, look for low-cost adventures in your area. Another tip is to pack lunch to avoid the cost to dine in restaurants. Of course, if you are a foodie, you will need to plan for your dining experiences. There is a cost associated with traveling via bus, train, uber, etc. If you can head out on foot to the event, this will save on transportation costs. Sometimes, there is a need to just hop in a cab and go.

It's a balance. Start small. Don't overwhelm yourself. Do you want to spend $20 per month, $50 per month? Or do you want to take advantage of "freemiums"? Do what is best for you. If you will need to postpone an event or cancel due to budget constraints, it's okay. Just plan to do something else. What's cool about this experiment is that you can change the formula to meet your needs.

Tip 2: Real Talk, the Gear!

Okay. You are now an adventurer, so you will need some essentials to help you navigate the world. Consider that you will be subject to all elements: rain, sleet, snow, and wind. When I decided to launch this experiment, I had to think like a hiker climbing Mount Everest.

Since you are venturing out into the world, you will need to quickly change clothes so that you are comfortable on your journey. A lot of companies have relaxed on the dress code. We are a blue-jean culture, so this was helpful for me. Instead of wearing a pair of dress slacks or a skirt, I could dress up a pair of jeans for work and then throw on a t shirt or sweatshirt before heading out. Take a moment to evaluate your adventure gear. Do you have a multipurpose bag? Do you have a comfortable pair of walking shoes? How about an umbrella?

I converted to living a minimalistic lifestyle, so function is more important for me than fashion. First, I threw away my tote bag. A tote bag did not fit the criteria for a traveler's bag. I needed one good weatherproof bag. A bag that could hold my laptop, flip flops, a change of clothes, lunch, and other travel essentials. So I purchased a backpack. Secondly, I converted all my work pants to blue jeans. Finally, I upgraded my shoe game. Walking around town, hopping on trolleys and on-and-off boats is difficult wearing heels or flats. So I invested in a good pair of walking shoes. In summary, I purchased a lot of cotton. Cotton is a breathable material that you can wear anywhere.

Here is what you will need to prepare for your journey:

1. Walking shoes
2. Foldable selfie stick

3. Folding camera tripod
4. Cellphone and charger
5. Functional bag or backpack
6. Flip flops
7. First-aid kit
8. Umbrella or poncho

Tip 3: Start a Movement

Let's start a movement. The goal is to create a community of individuals that want to live deliberately. I would love to see a day when thousands are walking out of the concrete jungle to live life in color. We can start by sharing these ideas with a friend. We can hold each other accountable. Why do we have to live our lives in bondage? I see a future where we negotiate more time off during the workday!

Freedom to take the time needed to take care of ourselves. If I can help just one person draw a line in the sand and say, "Enough is enough," then I have done what God put me here to do. At the end of the thirty-day experiment, I cried. I knew that my body and soul needed this. My eyes were brighter; I was happier, free.

It starts by changing the global definition of a workday. Did you know that Americans have the least amount of time off? It's true. The World Health Organization (WHO) has officially recognized "burnout" as a health condition. The movement will become effective when employees negotiate longer breaks. A thirty-minute or one-hour break per day is simply not enough. The only thing that you can really do is grab a sandwich, then back to work.

If employees are allowed more flexibility to explore and learn during the workday, this could increase productivity. This archaic idea regarding of what a break should look like is replicated millions of times across the globe. During the job offer process, "deliberate lunchers" should negotiate longer breaks. More time off for vacations is okay, but what about the time that you are losing during the workweek?

How we can start a movement to "disrupt the workday"?

1. Share this idea with a friend.
2. Start a blog to share experiences.
3. Hold each other accountable.
4. Take control of the hours in our workday.
5. Negotiate longer breaks during job offer process.
6. Start an experiment in the workplace.

The Next Chapter

I feel like this journey is never-ending. Living deliberately will always be a part of my life. If you are thinking, What is next for me? Well, there were some things that I did not have a chance to do.

Squeezing everything into thirty days was crazy. I knew that I would need to plan for the next chapter. I already have some things in motion. More to come. When I look at my list of what I want to experience, I'm excited to head out and see what I missed. I did not have a chance to see the artwork along the train route. I did not make it to a blues or jazz set. I still have not experienced my first poetry slam. I recaptured more than thirty hours of my life, living more deliberately. Maybe the next time, I should increase it to sixty hours—no, a hundred hours away from the office.

Anything is possible! We live every day to prove that we are not who are perceived to be.

I will see you in the next series.

I had to remember that the goal was to gain control over the clock and not to let the clock control me.

—Teri McElrath

ABOUT THE AUTHOR

Teri McElrath is an entrepreneur, author, and creator of the blog *Deliberate Luncher*. She currently resides in Chicago, Illinois, with an extended community of friends and family. Teri graduated from Loyola University on the north side of Chicago. She holds a BA in political science. Teri also holds an MA in human services and an MHRM in human resources. Her career spans more than twenty years as a human resource professional for *Fortune 500* companies in Chicago.

Teri's favorite destination is Chicago's lakefront. In her free time, she enjoys learning new things, dancing, and spending time with friends and family. She also enjoys poetry, art, documentaries, and road trips.

Disrupt the Workday is a culmination of entries from Teri's journal, originally sketched art, inspirational daily quotes, and a call to action to readers to "live deliberately."

The book was designed to be a total immersive experience for the reader. Teri creatively incorporates storytelling and visuals to create a unique experience for those who dare to take the journey.

To connect with Teri:
Blog: https://deliberateluncher.home.blog
Email: contact@deliberateluncher.com

CPSIA information can be obtained
at www.ICGtesting.com
Printed in the USA
BVHW021339231121
622333BV00022B/674

9 781638 440086